The Call to Discipleship

FACETS

Other Titles in the Facets Series

The Call
to Discipleship

Karl Barth

Translated by G. W. Bromiley

Edited by K. C. Hanson

Fortress Press
Minneapolis

THE CALL TO DISCIPLESHIP

Fortress Press Facets edition 2003

Scripture passages are from the New Revised Standard Version of the Bible, copyright © 1946, 1952, 1971, 1989 by the Division of Christian Education of the National Council of the Churches of Christ in the USA. Used by permission.

This volume is an excerpt from: Karl Barth, *Church Dogmatics*, vol. 4, pt. 2: *The Doctrine of Reconciliation*, translated by G. W. Bromiley (Edinburgh: T. & T. Clark, 1958). The original edition is *Die Kirchliche Dogmatik*, vol. 4, pt. 2: *Die Lehre von der Versöhnung* (Zollikon: Evangelischer Verlag, 1956).

Cover photo © Doug Plummer/Superstock. Used by permission.
Typesetting: Abby Coles

ISBN 0-8006-3632-5

The paper used in this publication meets the minimum requirements of American National Standard for Information Sciences—Permanence of Paper for Printed Library Materials, ANSI Z329.48-1984.

Manufactured in the U.S.A.

Contents

Editor's Note

From his commentary on Romans to his survey of Protestant theology in the nineteenth century, Karl Barth's writings had a deep impact on the theology of the twentieth century. But his vast *Church Dogmatics* stands as his foundational work.

The present volume is a brief excerpt from *Church Dogmatics* (vol. 4, pt. 2). In it, the author articulates his understanding of what it means to be called to follow Jesus.

Readers should note that I have edited Prof. Geoffrey W. Bromiley's translation in a few minor ways. The original translation was done for T. & T. Clark (Edinburgh), and thus British conventions of spelling and citation were employed. I have changed these to comport with U.S. conventions for this edition. I have also provided English renderings of Hebrew, Greek, and Latin words and phrases. And since the author makes repeated reference to Dietrich Bonhoeffer's *Discipleship* (originally published in English as *The Cost of Discipleship*), I have employed the new Fortress Press edition: *Discipleship*, edited by Geffrey B. Kelly and John D. Godsey, translated by Barbara Green and Reinhard Krauss, Dietrich Bonhoeffer Works 4 (Minneapolis: Fortress Press, 2001). I have attempted to make the language more gender-inclusive as well. For biblical quotations, the NRSV is employed here. I have added a few notes at the end for clarification and a brief list of books for further reading.

—K. C. Hanson

1
Introduction

"Follow me" is the substance of the call in the power of which Jesus makes people his saints. It is to this concreteness of his action that we must now turn. The lifting up of themselves for which he gives them freedom is not a movement which is formless, or to which they themselves have to give the necessary form. It takes place in a definite form and direction. Similarly, their looking to Jesus as their Lord is not an idle gaping. It is a vision that stimulates those to whom it is given to a definite action. <u>The call issued by Jesus is a call to discipleship</u>.

We must not waste time describing and criticizing that which, in adoption of very earlier traditions, the later Middle Ages and certain Protestant trends understood and attempted as an "imitation of Christ" *(imitatio Christi)*.[1] The matter is well enough known. It involves

1

a program in which we try to shape our lives by the example of the life of Jesus as sketched in the gospels and the commandments that he gave to his own people and to all people generally. And the objections to it are obvious, and therefore facile. It will be more instructive for our present purpose if we turn at once to the problem that is unavoidably posed by these movements, and especially by the New Testament itself. The discussion of this problem will enable us to weigh both critically and positively the doctrine and exercise of the *imitatio Christi*.

Easily the best that has been written on this subject is to be found in *Discipleship*, by Dietrich Bonhoeffer.[2] We do not refer to all the parts, that were obviously compiled from different sources, but to the opening sections, "The Call to Discipleship," "Simple Obedience" (omitted in the earlier English-language editions), and "Discipleship and the Individual." In these the matter is handled with such depth and precision that I am almost tempted simply to reproduce them in an extended quotation. For I cannot hope to say anything better on the subject than what is said here by a man who, having written on discipleship, was ready to achieve it in his own life, and did in his own way achieve it even to the point of death. In following my own course, I am happy that on this occasion I can lean as heavily as I do upon another.

Before we take up the problem as such, it may be as well to consider briefly what is to be learned linguistically from the biblical use of the decisive Greek term *akolouthein*. In this respect I am indebted to Gerhard Kittel's article.[3]

Akolouthein means "to go after or behind someone." Rather strangely, the Old Testament used the corresponding word mostly as a kind of technical term for the sinful pursuit of other gods. This gave to the word a pejorative sense, and Jer 2:2 is perhaps the only occasion that we read of a following of Yahweh:

> I remember the devotion of your youth,
>   your love as a bride,
> how you followed me in the wilderness,
>   in a land not sown.

The rabbis doubted, indeed, whether there could be any following of God at all in the sense of a following of God

himself, of his *shekinah* (presence). For
God is far too transcendent. As they saw
it (in a striking parallel to the Greek idea
of the similarity that a person achieves
with God by approaching *[epesthai]* as
one acts like him), it is a matter of following the qualities or acts of God:

- planting the land as God did the
  Garden of Eden
- clothing the naked as God clothed
  Adam
- visiting the sick as God did Abraham
- comforting the sad as God did Isaac
- burying the dead as God did Moses.

In this we have almost an early form
of the later Christian idea of *imitatio*. For
the rest, the Old Testament and rabbis
offer us only the "following" (which has
no theological significance) of honored
leaders. The warrior follows his captain,
the wife her husband, the bride her bride-
groom, the son of the prophet his master,
the scholar the rabbi who goes or rides before him on an ass. It is this that leads us
to the New Testament with its thought of
following Jesus. This occurs only in the
four gospels (with the exception of Rev
14:4); and in the first instance it envisages

an external going after him, the word being apparently limited to this sense in such passages as Mark 3:7, etc., where we are told that "a great multitude followed him." Following as they practiced it, it had both an inward and an outward limit.

Yet there were others—and it is here that the word acquires its pregnant meaning—who are called by Jesus and follow him in the sense that they accompany him wholeheartedly and constantly, sharing his life and destiny at the expense of all other engagements and commitments, attaching themselves to him, placing themselves in his service, and thus showing that they are qualified to be his disciples; not as though the messianic salvation is ascribed only to them, or even to them in particular, but as those who particularly attest and proclaim it. Their qualification as disciples, and therefore for discipleship, in this pregnant sense, is a gift, a "being fit" *(euthetos einai)* for the kingdom of God (Luke 9:62), a capacity with which they are endowed. Normally the fact that they are endowed in this way means also that they accompany him. Yet there are some qualified disciples who do not do so, and on the other hand there are others who accompany him but are not qualified disciples in this sense. It is worth noting in conclusion that the New Testament never uses the substantive "discipleship" *(akolouthēsis)* but only the verb "follow" *(akolouthein)* or "follow after me" *(opisō mou erchesthai).* This is a warning that in our consideration of this question we must always remember that we are dealing with what is obviously on the New Testament view an event that cannot be enclosed in a general concept. The further implications of discipleship must be developed from concrete passages within this wider context.

2
Grace in the Form of Command

We will again begin by stating that the call to discipleship is the particular form of the summons by which Jesus discloses and reveals himself to individuals in order to claim and sanctify them as his own, and as his witness in the world. It has the form of a command of Jesus directed to them. It means the coming of grace, for what is disclosed and revealed in Jesus is the reconciliation of the world with God as his reconciliation and therefore the fulness of salvation. But as it encounters them in this summons, grace has the form of command, the Gospel the form of the Law. The grace that comes to them requires that they could do something, i.e., follow Jesus. It is thus a grace that commands. Jesus is seeking people to serve him. He has already found them to the extent that he has elected them as

7

ordained to this end. They are already his people even as he claims them. He thus establishes his particular relationship to them by commanding them. He does this in his authority as the Son of Man who is their Lord, who can thus dispose concerning them, who has already done so, and who addresses them accordingly. Both Jeremiah and Paul understood that even from the mother's womb they were ordained for the action commanded. Jesus is already the Lord of those whom he calls to follow. He calls them as such. He commands them as those who already belong to him. This is what constitutes the overwhelming force of his command. This is why there can be no legitimate opposition to it. This is why there can be no question of any presuppositions on the part of those who are called: of any capacity or equipment for the performance of what is commanded; of any latent faith; of any inward or outward preparation. This is why there can be no question or self-selection on the part of those who follow. This is why those who are called cannot think of laying down conditions on which they are prepared to obey his command. Just because the command of

Jesus is the form of the grace that concretely comes to person, it is issued with all the freedom and sovereignty of grace against which there can be no legitimate objections, of which no one is worthy, for which there can be no preparation, which none can elect, and in face of which there can be no qualifications.

Disobedience to the command of Jesus: "Follow me," as in the case of the rich young ruler in Mark 10:17-18 and parallels, is a phenomenon that is absolutely terrifying in its impossibility. It provokes the question of the disciples: "Who then can be saved?" For in it there is revealed the far too common rule of the natural, or unnatural, attitude of humanity to this command. In the light of the command of Jesus given to a person, disobedience is inconceivable, inexplicable, and impossible. On the other hand, we might ask who is the man Levi that when Jesus sees him at the receipt of custom (Mark 2:14-15) he should at once issue the same command: "Follow me?" How much we should have to read into the short account if we were to try to explain from Levi himself, and his moral and religious qualifications, why it is that he is given this command and proceeds at once to execute it. We can only abandon the attempt. The secret of Levi is that of the one who calls him. Again, we are told in Luke 9:57-58 about a man who met Jesus in the way with the offer: "I will follow you wherever you go." He is obviously one who has presumed to do this on his own initiative. And his answer is the terrible saying about the foxes that have holes, and the birds of the air nests, "but the Son of Man—whom he is going to follow—hath not where to lay his head." He does not realize that it is that he thinks he can choose. He does not know how terrible is the venture to which he commits himself in the execution of this choice.

No one of themselves can or will imagine that this is their way, or take this way. What Jesus wills with his "Follow me" can be chosen only in obedience to his call. We can see this from the saying of Peter: "Lord, if it is you, command me to come to you on the water" (Matt 14:28). Without being bidden by Christ, he could not do this. It has also been noted that there can be no conditions. The man mentioned in Luke 9:61-62 lacked true discipleship, not merely because he offered it to Jesus as a matter for his own choice, but because he also made a condition: "Let me first say farewell to those at my home." Those who offer themselves to be disciples are obviously bound to be of the opinion that they can lay down the conditions on which they will do this. But a limited readiness is no readiness at all in our dealings with Jesus. It is clear that this man, too, does not really know what he thinks he has chosen. It is certainly not the following of Jesus. This is commanded unconditionally, and therefore it cannot be entered upon except unconditionally. The answer of Jesus makes it quite plain that this person cannot be considered as a disciple: "No one who puts a hand to the plow and looks back is fit for the kingdom of God."

3
Bound to the One Who Calls

The call to discipleship binds a person to the One who calls him. He is not called by an idea of Christ, or a Christology, or a christocentric system of thought, let alone the supposedly Christian conception of a Father-God. How could these call him to discipleship? They have neither words nor voice. They cannot bind anyone to themselves. We must be careful that we do not conceal the living Jesus behind such schemata, fearing that the one who can issue this call, who has the words and voice to do it, and above all the right and authority and power to bind, might actually do so.

Again, discipleship is not the recognition and adoption of a programme, ideal or law, or the attempt to fulfill it. It is not the execution of a plan of individual or social construction imparted and commended by Jesus. If the word "discipleship" is in any

way used to denote something general and
not a concrete and therefore a concretely
filled-out event between Jesus and this
particular person, the command "Follow
me" can only be described as quite mean-
ingless. For the only possible content of
this command is that this or that specific
person to whom it is given should come to,
and follow, and be with, the one who gives
it. In this one, and the relationship that it
establishes between him and the one he
calls, a good deal more is involved. But
there is nothing apart from him and this relationship.

That a person should come to him is
the one complete work that one is called
to do. We may say, therefore, that in
practice the command to follow Jesus is
identical with the command to believe in
him. It demands that a person who as
such brings no other presuppositions
than that one is entangled like all other
people in the general sloth of humanity,
and has to suffer the consequences,
should put one's trust in God as the God
who is faithful to the unfaithful, who in
spite of their own forgetfulness has not
forgotten them, who without any cooper-
ation or merit on their part wills that they

should live and not die. In the call of
Jesus one is met by the fulfilled promise
of God as valid for her or him. In and
with the command of Jesus, solid ground
is placed under their feet when they are
on the point of falling into the abyss.
What the command requires of them is
simply, but comprehensively, that in
practice as well as in theory they should
regard it as able to bear him, and stand
on it, and no longer leave it.

This is what we do when we trust; and
in so doing we do all that is required of
us. To do this is to believe. But in the faith
here required we do not have a trust in
the abstract or in general, nor do we have
the rash confidence of a hazardous journey into space. It is demanded by Jesus—
the Son of Man who as the Son of God
speaks in the name and with the full authority of God. And what Jesus demands
is trust in himself and therefore, in the
concrete form that this involves, trust in
God. He demands faith in the form of
obedience; obedience to himself. This is
the commitment to him that constitutes
the content of the call to discipleship. We
cannot separate any one moment of this
event from any of the others. That he, the

Son of Man who is the Son of the Father, lives and rules as the lord of all men; that as the savior of all people he comes to a particular person, who is as little worthy of it as any others, to make himself known to that person as the one who is also his savior; that in so doing he simply claims him for himself as one of his, and for his service; that he thus demands of that person faith in God and trust in himself; that the faith demanded of this person includes the obedience that has to be rendered to Jesus: all these are inseparable moments of the one event.

There is no discipleship without the one who calls to it. There is no discipleship except as faith in God as determined by the One who calls to it and frees for it. There is no discipleship that does not consist in the act of the obedience of this faith in God and therefore in him.

It is with these contours that the call to discipleship goes out as recorded and attested in the Gospels. Everything depends upon the fact that Jesus himself is there and lives and calls people to himself. We are never told what his will is for Levi or Simon Peter, or the others whom he calls. Nor is any attempt made to establish or explain his authority to call them. It is enough for the evangelists in their description of the origin of the disciple-relationship, and it must obviously be enough for us too in our understanding of it, that Jesus does actually call them, and call them to himself. He summons them. They are to give to him the faith of which God is worthy and which is owed to him; the faith and therefore the confidence that they are helped by him and therefore by God; that within the world of human sloth and its consequences they are helped to overcome these and to be set up: "Whoever follows me will never walk in darkness but will have the light of life" (John 8:12). Or, as we are told of the 144,000 "who follow the Lamb wherever he goes," they are the first fruits of the redeemed from among people, and they bear his name and the name of his Father in their foreheads, and they sing a new song before the throne (Rev 14:1-4).

His summons is, however, that they should give to him and therefore to God a true and serious and total faith: not a mere acceptance of the fact that he is their Lord nor an idle confidence that they are helped by him; but this accept-ance and confidence as a faith that is lived out and practiced by them; a faith that is proved to be a true and serious faith by the fact that it includes at once their obedience—what Paul called the "obedience of faith" *(hupakoē pisteōs)* in Rom 1:5 and 16:26, and "obey Christ" *(hupakoē tou Christou)* in 2 Cor 10:5. "Why do you call me 'Lord, Lord,' and do not do what I tell you?" (Luke 6:46). There can be no doubt that what moved those who were called to be disciples as they followed the call of Jesus was simply their faith in him as the Lord, and there-fore in God. But it was a faith that at once impelled them to obedience. There is nothing in the accounts of the call of the disciples to suggest a kind of interval, i.e., that they first believed in him, and then decided to obey him, and actually did so. It is never an open question whether, when and how obedience has to begin if faith is presupposed.

Faith is not obedience, but as obedi-ence is not obedience without faith, faith is not faith without obedience. They be-long together, as do thunder and lightning in a thunderstorm. Levi would not have obeyed if he had not arisen and followed Jesus. The fishermen by the lake would not have believed if they had not immediately *(euthus)* left their nets and followed him. Peter on the lake would not have believed if he had not obeyed Jesus' call to come, and left the boat and gone to him on the water (Matt 14:29). But Peter and all of them did believe, and therefore they did at once and self-evidently that which was commanded. It is true that in the continuation of the story Peter looked at the raging wind instead of Jesus, and was afraid, and doubted, and could go no farther, but could only sink, and would have sunk if he had not been gripped by the hand of the one in whom he had so little faith. But this only shows that the disciple cannot obey without believing, or conversely that when he believes he must and can obey, and actually does so.

4
Taking a Step in Faith

The call to discipleship, no matter how
or when it is issued to someone, or
whether it comes to a person for the first
time or as a second or third or hundredth
confirmation, is always the summons to
take in faith, without which it is impossible, a definite first step. This step, as one
that is taken in faith, i.e., faith in Jesus, as
an act of obedience to him, is distinguished from every other step that one
may take by the fact that in relation to
the whole of one's previous life and
thinking and judgment it involves an
about-turn and therefore a complete
break and new beginning. To follow Jesus
means to go beyond oneself in a specific
action and attitude, and therefore to turn
one's back upon oneself, to leave oneself
behind. That this is the case may and will
not always be equally perceptible from
the particular step, the particular action
or attitude, which is demanded as the act
of faith. But—however imperceptible that

which we do may be—it can never be a question of a routine continuation or repetition of what has hitherto been our customary practice. It always involves the decision of a new day; the seizing of a new opportunity that was not present yesterday but is now given in and with the call of Jesus. Inevitably, people who are called by Jesus renounce and turn away from themselves as they were yesterday. To use the important New Testament expression, they deny themselves.

Where it is used in a pregnant sense, and not merely of a simple denial, *arneisthai* always denotes in the New Testament the renunciation, withdrawal, and annulment of an existing relationship of obedience and loyalty. Peter denies that he was ever with Jesus of Nazareth: "I do not know or understand what you are saying" (Mark 14:68 and par.). The Jews deny Jesus, their own Messiah, the Servant of God, in the presence of Pilate (Acts 3:13). There are also ostensible, but in reality anti-Christian, Christians who deny the Lord who bought them (2 Pet 2:1). In particular, they deny that Jesus is the Christ, thus making themselves guilty of a denial of

the Father and the Son (1 John 2:22).
John the Baptist denies that he himself is
the Messiah (John 1:20), and in so doing
he does not deny, but indirectly recog-
nizes, that Jesus is. Denial is the opposite
of confession *(homolegeisthai)*, in which
a person stands both in word and deed to
a relationship of obedience and loyalty
in which he finds himself.

The disciple who does not do this to
others in respect of his relationship to
Jesus—"Those who are ashamed of me
and of my words in this adulterous and
sinful generation" (Mark 8:38)—denies
him as Peter did; and this automatically
means that so long and to the extent that
one does this the relationship of Jesus to
him or her, his advocacy for him or her
before God, is dissolved: "I will also deny
[them] before my Father in heaven" (Matt
10:33, cf. 2 Tim 2:12). This is the objec-
tive factor in the bitterness experienced
by Peter in consequence of his denial. In
the same sense, and with the menace of
the same dreadful consequences, there is
a denial of the name of Jesus (Rev 3:8) or
of his faith (*pistis;* Rev 2:13). It is re-
markable that the same verb which in this
pregnant sense denotes the most dreadful

thing of which the disciple can conceivably be guilty in his relationship to Jesus is also used (although this time with reference to himself) to describe the peak point in this relationship, the characteristic turning of obedience.

In 2 Tim 2:13 the culminating reason for the impossibility of denying Christ as the Christian sees it is the fact that "he cannot deny himself"—for how can the Son of Man deny that he is the Son of God? But at the decisive point in the Synoptics, the very opposite is true of ourselves: "If any want to become my followers, let them deny themselves" (*aparnēsasthō eauton;* Mark 8:34). The idea is exactly the same. The person who is called to follow Jesus has simply to renounce and withdraw and annul an existing relationship of obedience and loyalty. This relationship is to oneself. When one is called to discipleship, one abandons oneself resolutely and totally. One can and must say of oneself instead of Jesus: "I do not know the man" (Matt 26:72). One cannot accept this person even as one's most distant acquaintance. One once stood in a covenant with him or her that one loyally kept and tenderly nurtured. But one now renounces this covenant root and branch. One can confess only Jesus, and therefore cannot confess oneself. One can and will only deny oneself.

But in the context of discipleship to Jesus, which is a definite event, that is a very definite step. It is not merely a new and critical and negative mind and attitude in relation to oneself. This will also be involved. But in and for itself, in the uncommitted sphere of inwardness, this might be present without the definite loosing of a person from herself or himself, and therefore without a definite act of obedience. In this case discipleship would only be theoretical. It would not be an actual event. The call to discipleship would not have really reached and affected the person, or that one would have imprisoned and tamed and rendered it innocuous in the sphere of emotion or reflection. An inner withdrawal from oneself is not by a long way a breach of the covenant or denial of acquaintance with oneself, and therefore self-denial in the sense of discipleship. In itself and as such, if this is the whole of the matter, it might be the most radical and obstinate denial of this breach or renunciation. Indeed, where this is the whole of the matter, it will certainly be the case.

Self-denial in the context of following Jesus involves a step into the open, into the freedom of a definite decision and act, in which it is with a real commitment that person takes leave of himself or herself, of the person of yesterday, of the person she or he was; in which one gives up the previous form of one's existence, hazarding and totally compromising oneself without looking back or considering what is to become of herself or himself, because what matters is not now oneself but that one should do at all costs that which is proposed and demanded, having no option but to decide and act in accordance with it—cost what it may. "For God's sake do something brave," was once the cry of Ulrich Zwingli (1484–1531) to his contemporaries. Not feel, or think, or consider, or meditate! Not turn it over in your heart and mind! But *do* something brave. If it is to this that Jesus calls a person in his discipleship, there can be no avoiding genuine self-denial.

To be sure, we have not merely to do anything that is brave, or that smacks of bravery. Even though we might find precedents for it in history, or Church history, or the Bible, a mere act of bravery might well be performed without self-denial. Indeed, it might even be an act of supreme self-assertion. For all his sloth, the old Adam whom we have to leave behind loves sometimes to emerge in great acts. It is a matter of doing that which is proposed to us by Jesus. It may be great or it may be small. It may be striking or it may be insignificant. But its performance is laid upon us, not by ourselves, but by the one who has called us to himself, who has willed and chosen us as his own. And we are to perform it in the act of that obedience which cannot be separated from faith in him.

As a person renders this obedience, one will certainly not be able to assert oneself. One can only deny oneself. The call with which Jesus calls and binds a person to himself means that one should leave everything that yesterday, and even yet, might seem self-evident and right and good and useful and promising. It also means that we should leave a merely inward and mental movement in which we do not really do anything, but only speechifies in an idle dialectic, in mere deliberations and projects concerning what we might do but cannot and will not yet do, because we have not yet reached the point of action in our consideration of it and of the situation in which it is to be done. We take leave of both, for in both the old Adam is enthroned—the self whom we have to deny in the discipleship of Jesus.

This Adam is denied in the new act demanded by the call of Jesus, and the brave thing demanded of his disciples consists in what Dietrich Bonhoeffer calls "simple obedience."[4] Obedience is simple when we do just what we are told—nothing more, nothing less, and nothing different. In simple obedience we *do* it, and therefore we do not finally not do it. But what we do is literally and exactly that which we are commanded to do. The only possible obedience to Jesus' call to discipleship is simple obedience in these two senses. This alone is rendered in self-denial. This alone is the brave act of faith in Jesus.

Bonhoeffer is ten times right when at this point he inveighs sharply against a theological interpretation of the given command and the required obedience which is to the effect that the call of Jesus is to be heard but his command may be taken to mean that the obedience required will not necessarily take the form of the act which is obviously demanded but may in certain cases consist in the neglect of this act and the performance of others which are quite different.

This interpretation may be stated as follows. The command of Jesus is naturally to be heard and accepted and followed with joy. It is the commanding grace of God, and therefore the salvation of the whole world and of humanity, entering life as a free offer. How can we resist it?

But what does it mean to follow? What is commanded is obviously that we should come to Jesus; that we should believe in him as God; that he should believe in God by believing in him; that we should trust him wholly and utterly; that we should be willing and ready, therefore, for every hazard or venture or sacrifice that in a given situation might prove to be necessary to confirm this trust. Yet as concerns the concrete form of the command of Jesus, in which we have to do with something definite that we are commanded to do or not do, this concrete thing is only designed more sharply to describe and emphasize the totality and depth with which the command requires faith, and with faith the willingness and readiness for what may in certain circumstances be the supreme and most perfect sacrifice.

Obedience to it means an inward liberation from everything in which we might otherwise put our trust; the loosening of all other ties to the point of being able to sever them at any moment. We need not do precisely what the command of Jesus explicitly demands. The point of the explicit command is the implicit—that we should believe, and that in our faith we should be alert to do either that which is explicitly commanded or something similar and along the same lines. When we have accepted that which is implied in the command, we have already obeyed in the true sense. We have "as though we had not." By what is meant in the command, and the willingness and readiness we bring to it, everything else that we have is radically called in question.

We do everything only "as though we did it not." Inwardly, therefore, we are free. We are free even perhaps to do that which is explicitly commanded. But do we

have to do it? No, for that would be a legalistic interpretation of the command,
which even in what seems to be its concrete demand that we should do this or
that is really calling us only to the freedom in which we may do it but do not
have to do so. On a true and proper interpretation the command of Jesus does not
command us to do this specific thing.
There is no question of having to do it. In
obedience to the command we may just as
well do something else and even the very
opposite. For example, instead of giving
all that we have to the poor, we may
maintain and increase our possessions; or
instead of turning the other cheek, we
may return the blow that we have received. All, of course, "as though we did it
not!" All in a willingness and readiness
one day perhaps—when the opportunity
and situation offer—to do that which is
concretely demanded! All on a true and
spiritual understanding, and in a genuine
exercise, of the obedience of faith! All in a
grateful appropriation of the salvation
which comes with Jesus' call to discipleship! But with the result that for the moment that which Jesus literally asks
remains undone, and the outward state

and course of affairs remains unchanged by his command and our obedience.

Bonhoeffer's commentary on this line of thought and its result is as follows:

> Anywhere else in the world where commands are given, the situation is clear. A father says to his child: go to bed! The child knows exactly what to do. But a child drilled in pseudotheology would have to argue thus: Father says go to bed. He means you are tired; he does not want me to be tired. But I can also overcome my tiredness by going to play. So, although father says go to bed, what he really means is go play. With this kind of argumentation, a child with its father or a citizen with the authorities would run into an unmistakable response, namely, punishment. The situation is supposed to be different only with respect to Jesus' command.[5]

The ghost of this interpretation cannot be too quickly laid. The commanding grace of God, and therefore salvation as

Jesus' call to discipleship, never come into the life of a person in such a way that one is given leave to consider why and how one may best follow the command given. The command given is recognizable as the command of Jesus by the fact that it is quite unambiguous. It required to be fulfilled only as it is given—and one's reception or non-reception of salvation depends upon whether this is done or not. The faith that Jesus actually demands is not just a radical readiness and willingness for all contingencies—a kind of supply which is there to draw upon as required but is stored up for the time being. It is distinguished as trust in Jesus, and therefore as genuine trust in God, by the fact that as it is given to persons and grasped by them it at once takes on the form of the definite resolve and act indicated by the call of Jesus.

The command given to a person by Jesus is not given to the one who receives it in such a way that he may freely distinguish between what is meant and what is willed, between the implicit content and the explicit form, the former being accepted but the latter provisionally ignored. It has its content only in its specific form. Only as it turns to the latter can it keep seriously to the former. Again, it is not the case that in obedience to the call of Jesus we can and should and even (in all prudence) must postpone a full inward and outward rendering of it until we find a favourable opportunity and situation; the psychological, historical, economic or political situation indispensable to its integral achievement. To be sure, we for our part have not to create a situation of this kind. But we have to realize that the command of Jesus given us itself creates the situation and all the conditions of the situation in which we have to obey, so that there is no place for any further waiting for a developing situation or suitable moment, nor for any further consideration, appraisal or selection of different possibilities, but only for instant obedience. In obedience we are not about to leap. We are already leaping.

The line of argument which we have been reconstructing has, of course, a ring of profundity. It seems to give a triumphant answer to monks and fanatics and other legalists. But this is an illusion. It is not simple obedience that is legalistic, but the arbitrarily discursive and dialectical obedience which evades the command. It is the disobedience, disguised as obedience, of a flight into inwardness at the point where the inward person can and should express himself or herself outwardly. It is the disobedience of the flight into faith at the point where faith as the obedience of the heart relentlessly involves the obedience of action.

It is not from the concrete command of Jesus that there comes the threat of the Law to whose dominion we must no longer subject ourselves; it is from the forced conceptions in the light of which we think we can arbitrarily release ourselves from concrete obedience to the concrete command of Jesus. Those who acted legalistically were not the fishers by the lake who at the bidding of Jesus left the nets and followed him, but men like the rich young ruler who when he heard what he had to do "he was shocked and went away grieving, for he had many possessions" (Mark 10:22). If we will not bear the yoke of Jesus, we have to bear the yoke we ourselves have chosen, and it is a hundred times more heavy. The attitude corresponding to that line of argument has nothing whatever to do with the true flight to Jesus. On the contrary, it is a flight from him. <u>We refuse to take the first step towards him, and therefore we cannot take any further steps.</u> Where we undertake the flight to him, it is inevitable that in and with the first step demanded not merely the outer but the inner state and course of our lives and therefore our surroundings will be affected and in some way basically altered. The call of Jesus makes history when it is heard and taken seriously. It is by this that we may know whether or not it is heard; whether or not it is heard and taken seriously as a call to self-denial.

5
Making a Break

The call to discipleship makes a break. It is not the obedient person who does it, not even with simple obedience. What one does in this obedience can only be an indication of this break. If one is not to be disobedient, what option does one have but to do as one is told? But good care is taken—and one has to realize the fact—that in one's action one can never accomplish more than an indication, demonstration and attestation of this break. It is the call of Jesus, going out into the world and accepted by that one, which makes the break; which has already made it.

The kingdom of God is revealed in this call; the kingdom which is among the kingdoms of this world, but which confronts and contradicts and opposes them; the *coup d'etat* of God proclaimed and accomplished already in the existence of the man Jesus. The person whom Jesus calls to himself has to stand firm by the revelation of it. Indeed, that one has to correspond to it in what one does and does not do. His or her own action, if it is obedient, will always attest and indicate it. It will not do this in accordance with his or her own judgment or pleasure. It will do it in the way commanded. But because it is the man Jesus who causes them to do what they do, it will attest and indicate only this revelation. It may do so to a smaller or lesser degree. It may do so in strength or in weakness. But always it will set forth the kingdom of God drawn near, and therefore the greatest, the only true and definitive break in the world and its history as it has already taken place in Jesus Christ and cannot now be healed.

It is with this that we have to do in the discipleship of Jesus exercised in self-denial. While it is a matter of the personal self of the individual called by Jesus, of the dissolution of the covenant with himself or herself, the self-denial of the disciple is only a kind of culminating point in the great attack in which one is called to participate as one's witness, and which one has to recognize and support as in the first instance an attack upon oneself. If we are not ready to deny ourselves, of what use can we be as witnesses of the great assault that is directed against the world (for the sake of its reconciliation with God) in and with the coming of the kingdom? Our self-denial, and the first step which we are commanded to make by him who calls us, are not ends in themselves. They stand in the service of this great onslaught.

But in this onslaught it is a matter of God's destruction, accomplished in the existence of the Son of Man, of all the so-called "given factors," all the supposed natural orders, all the historical forces, which with the claim of absolute validity and worth have obtruded themselves as authorities—mythologically but very realistically described as "gods"—between God and humanity, but also between one person and another; or rather which inventive person has obtruded between God and oneself and oneself and other people. The dominion of these forces character-izes the world as the world of the slothful person. It continually makes it the world which strives against God, but which is for this very reason in a state of hopeless disintegration and in need of reconcilia-tion with God and of his peace. When they are posited absolutely, possessions (which are significantly described as "dishonest wealth" in Luke 16:9) and worldly honor, the force which defends them, the family with its claims and even the law of a religion (and worst of all a religion of revelation) are all gods which are first set up by humans, which are then worshipped in practice and which finally dominate them, interposing themselves between God and them, and between them and others, and maintaining themselves in this mediatorial position. It is not people, or any one person, who can make the break with these given factors and orders and historical forces. What a person does by oneself may take the form of an attempted repudiation but it will always serve to confirm and strengthen them, continually evoking new forms of their rule. The little revolutions and attacks by which they seem to be more shaken than they really are can never succeed even in limiting, let alone destroying, their power. It is the kingdom, the revolution, of God which breaks, which has already broken them. Jesus is their Conqueror.

If we are his disciples, we are necessarily witness of this fact. We are awakened by him from the dream that these forces are divine or divinely given actualities, eternal orders. We can no longer believe, and therefore we can no longer think or accept, that men, including ourselves, are indissolubly bound and unconditionally committed to them. In their place there stands for us the Conqueror Jesus, the one Mediator between God and humanity, and between one person and another; he who is the divine reality; he who decides what can and cannot be, what is and is not, a divinely given reality for us. If we are his disciples we are freed by him from their rule.

This does not mean that we are made superior, or set in a position of practical neutrality. It means that we can and must exercise our freedom in relation to them. It must be attested in the world as a declaration of the victory of Jesus. The world that sighs under these powers must hear and receive and rejoice that their lordship is broken. But this declaration cannot be made by the existence of those who are merely free inwardly. If the message is to be given, the world must see and hear at least an indication, or sign, of what has taken place. The break made by God in Jesus must become history. This is why Jesus calls his disciples.

And it is for this reason that his disciples cannot be content with a mere theory about the relativization of those false absolutes; a mere attitude of mind in which these gods no longer exist for them; and inward freedom in relation to them. It is for this reason that in different ways they are called out in practice from these attachments, and it is a denial of the call to discipleship if they evade the achievement of acts and attitudes in which even externally and visibly they break free from these attachments. They can never do this, in any respect, on their own impulse or according to their own caprice. It is not a matter of our own revolt, either as individuals or in company with those likeminded. It is a matter of the kingdom of God and God's revolution.

But the disciple of Jesus is always summoned to attest this in a specific way by one's own act and attitude. One has no right, nor is one free, to avoid the concretely given command. This is where we see the relevance of what we said about simple obedience above. There can be no question in self-denial of a soaring and tranquilizing mysticism of world-renunciation and freedom and conquest in which

the obligation to the godless and hostile orders already broken in Christ is not only
maintained but if anything validated and
sanctified. If this is all that is involved,
then no matter how profoundly or attrac-
tively it is present it is a highly irrelevant
enterprise. No, it is important only as, in
obedience to the one who demands it, it is
an indication of his attack and victory, and
therefore a concrete step out into the open
country of decision and act; of the decision
and act in which, even though he can only
indicate what is properly at issue, we can
only seem to be strange and foolish and
noxious to the world around us. Is it not
inevitable that in the first instance we will
have this appearance even to ourselves?
We must and will run the risk of being an
offence to those around us—and in so far as
we see with their eyes, to ourselves. We will
not seek or desire this. But we cannot avoid
the risk that it will be so. In relation to the
world he cannot, then, restrict ourselves to
an attempted "inner emigration" in which
we will not be offensive, or at least suspicious, or at the very least conspicuous, to
those who still worship their gods. It is not
merely a matter of saving our own souls in
the attainment of a private beatitude. We

lose our souls, and hazard our eternal salvation, if we will not accept the public re-
sponsibility which we assume when we
become disciples of Jesus. It is more than
doubtful whether we are doing this if our
existence does not force those around us to
take notice—with all the painful consequences this may involve for us. But they
will not take notice, nor will they be disturbed or annoyed by our existence, if we
do not come out into the open as who we
are, doing what they do not do, and not
doing what they do; if in our attitude to the
given factors and orders and historical
forces which they regard as absolute there
is no difference between us and them, but
only uniformity and conformity.

This may have the advantage for us
that we will not be disturbed or assailed by
them, but can live by our faith, and find
joy and even secret pride in what may perhaps be a very radical opposition in inward attitude. The only trouble is that we
will be quite useless as witnesses of the
kingdom of God. As a quiet participant in
the cause of this kingdom he will avoid
giving offence to anyone, but he will also
evade the obedience which we are required
to render. For this obedience necessarily

consists in the fact that publicly before those around us we take what is in a specific form a new path which leads us out of conformity with them to a place to which we specifically are pointed, so that to those who still persist in conformity we involuntarily but irresistibly makes ourselves conspicuous and suspicious and offensive, and can expect to meet with serious or petty forms of unpleasantness from them.

We will not provoke them. Like Daniel in the lions' den, he will be cautious not to pull the lions' tails. But we will encounter what we must encounter if God does not unexpectedly decree otherwise. We will have to endure it. It is better not to describe ourselves as warriors. If we are in our right senses, we will not think of ourselves as such. We does not go on his way out of conformity in opposition to any other men, but on behalf of all other men, as one who has to show them the liberation which has already taken place. The "army of Christ" *(militia Christi)* will arise of itself, although there can, of course, be no question of Christian contentiousness against non-Christians, let alone of violence, crusades, and the like. And even the *militia Christi* will not really consist in conflict against others, but decisively in conflict against oneself, and in the fact that one is assailed, and in some way has to suffer, and to accept suffering, at the hands of others. It is certainly not our commission to add to the sufferings of others, and therefore to fight against them.

Even for the sake of the kingdom of God which we are ordained to serve we need fight only by indicating, in what we do and do not do, the fact that it has dawned, that it has broken into the old world, so that visibly—and not just invisibly—we refuse respect and obedience to all the generally recognized and cultivated authorities and deities, not lifting our hats to the different governors set over us. We know that the battle against them is already won; that the victory over them is already an accomplished fact; that their power is already broken. Our task is perhaps offensive to others, but intrinsically it is the friendly and happy one of giving a practical indication of this fact. In its discharge we are concerned with the release and liberation of these others too. And we cannot escape this task.

At this point we must think of the concrete form of the demand with which Jesus in the Gospels always approached those whom he called to discipleship. It is common to every instance that the goal is a form of action or abstention by which his disciples will reveal and therefore indicate to the world the break in the human situation, the end of the irresistible and uncontested dominion of given factors and orders and historical forces, as it has been brought about by the dawn and irruption of the kingdom. It is common to every instance that the obedience concretely demanded of, and to be achieved by, the disciple, always means that he must move out of conformity with what he hitherto regarded as the self-evident action and abstention of Lord Everyman and into the place allotted to him, so that he is inevitably isolated in relation to those around him, not being able or willing to do in this place that which is generally demanded by the gods who are still fully respected in the world around. At this particular place he is freed from the bonds of that which is generally done or not done, because and as he is bound now to Jesus.

We must emphasize the "because and as." Except as one is directly bound to Jesus, a person is never called out of conformity with those around, and therefore loosed from the bonds of that which is generally done or not done. And this binding to Jesus must be thought of as a very particular matter—something which comes to each individual in a highly particular way in one's own particular time and situation. To *this* person he *now* gives—and this person now receives—*this* command as the concrete form of the call to discipleship now issued to him or her. It is not the case, then, that one is loosed from one general form of action, from the legalism of the world as determined by the dominion of those gods, only to be bound to the legalism of another generality, which simply consists in a radical, systematic, and consistent penetration and destruction of the first.

In face of the solid front of the action that is normative for the person of the world the commanding of Jesus does not establish what we might call the counterfront of an action which is normative for all his disciples in every age and situation. His bidding—and his is rather different—is

that in accordance with the direction
which he gives to each disciple in particular there should be different penetrations
of this front and the establishment of
signs of the kingdom in the world which
is ruled by the gods and subject to their
legalism. Thus, apart from himself as the
Lord, there is no new and revolutionary
law to which his disciples are no less subject than others are to the old law of the
cosmos dominated by these false absolutes. There is no such thing as a party
which is rallied by this law and that has to
contend for it as the parties of the divided
world have to fight for their different conceptions of the laws which rule the world.
There is only the new commanding of
Jesus in its relationship to this particular
person elected by him and in this particular time and situation which he has fixed.
This new commanding of his is the concrete form in which he calls these people,
here and now, to discipleship, and therefore sanctifies them.

It is clear that in the directions to discipleship and embodied in the Gospel
tradition we have to do with collective
accounts, even (and especially) where the
call is generally addressed to a majority

of his disciples or it may be to all of them. The fact that this was very quickly obscured led to the mistaken attempt to create out of these directions a new law *(nova lex)*, a general mode of Christian action in opposition to that of worldly action. The truth is, however, that what the Gospel sayings about the following of his disciples really preserve are certain prominent lines along which the concrete commanding of Jesus, with its demand for concrete obedience, always moved in relation to individuals, characterizing it as his commanding in distinction from that of all other lords. And these sayings are read aright by individuals who accept their witness that they too are called to obedience to the Lord who may be known as this Lord by the fact that his commanding, while it does not require the same thing of everyone, or even of the same person in every time and situation, always moves along one or more of these prominent lines. And the lines recorded in the Gospel all agree that person is always called to make a particular penetration of the front of the general action and abstention of others; to cut loose from a practical recognition

of the legalism determined by the dominion of worldly authorities.

Everything depends upon the fact
that it is Jesus who demands that we
make this penetration and cut loose in
this way. If this is not demanded, we can
be sure that it is not the command of
Jesus. And if it is not effected, we can be
sure that there is no obedience to him.
Even in action along the main lines of
the concrete forms of his demands there
can be no true action apart from a commitment to him, i.e., except as it is done
for his sake. Conversely, however, there
can be no commitment to him if the action of the disciple is not along one or
more of the great lines and if the freedom
of the kingdom of God is not attested—
this is the common element in every
case—to the imprisoned world in a visible
concretion.

Possessions

For us Westerners, at any rate, the most
striking of these main lines is that on
which Jesus, according to the Gospel
tradition, obviously commanded many
people, as the concrete form of their

obedient discipleship, to renounce their
general attachment to the authority, validity, and confidence of possessions,
not merely inwardly but outwardly, in
the venture and commitment of a definite act. We do not have here the real-
ization of an ideal or principle of
poverty as it was later assumed into the
monastic rule. Nor do we have the basis
of a new society freed from the principle
of private property. It is simply, but far
more incisively, a question of the specific summons to specific people, as in
Matt 5:42: "Give to everyone who begs
from you, and do not refuse anyone who
wants to borrow from you" (severely
sharpened in Luke 6:35: "Lend, expect-
ing nothing in return"); or in Matt 5:40:
"And if anyone wants to sue you and
take your coat, give your cloak as well";
or 6:31: "Therefore do not worry, saying,
'What will we eat?' or 'What will we
drink?' or 'What will we wear?'"; or
6:19: "Do not store up for yourselves
treasures on earth, where moth and rust
consume and where thieves break in and
steal"; or 6:24: "No one can serve two
masters. . . . You cannot serve God and
wealth;" or in the charge to the disciples

in Matt 10:9-10: "Take no gold, or silver, or copper in your belts, no bag for your journey, or two tunics, or sandals, or a staff; for laborers deserve their food"; or the demand, illustrated in the parable of the unjust steward, that we should make friends with the mammon of unrighteousness as long as we have it (Luke 16:9), and in this sense be "faithful" to it; or the radical command addressed to the rich young ruler whom Jesus loved: "You lack one thing; go, sell what you own, and give the money to the poor, and you will have treasure in heaven; then come, follow me" (Mark 10:21); and the echo in the words of Peter (Mark 10:28): "Look, we have left everything and followed you."

The line along which all this is said is obviously the same, although it cannot be reduced to a normative technical rule for dealing with possessions. On the contrary, it is palpable that these are specific directions given to specific men at specific times and to be specifically followed, not in a formalized or spiritualized, but a literal sense. The drift of them all is clearly that Jesus' call to discipleship challenges and indeed cuts right across the self-evident attachment to that which we possess. The man to whom the call of Jesus comes does not only think and feel but acts (here and now, in this particular encounter with his neighbour) as one who is freed from this attachment. We not only can but do let go that which is ours. By doing exactly as one is commanded by Jesus one successfully makes this sortie, attesting that the kingdom of mammon is broken by the coming of the kingdom of God.

Honor

Along a second line the instructions given by Jesus have to do no less directly with the destruction by the coming of the kingdom of what is generally accepted as honour or fame among men: "Blessed are you when people revile you and persecute you and utter all kinds of evil against you falsely on my account" (Matt 5:11). For "If they have called the master of the house Beelzebub, how much more will they malign those of his household" (Matt 10:25). And, therefore, "if anyone strikes you on the right cheek, turn the other also" (Matt 5:39). Or according to

The Call to Discipleship   53

the parable of the wedding-guests: "do
not sit down in the place of honor . . . but
at the lowest place . . . For all who exalt
themselves will be humbled, and those
who humble themselves will be exalted"
(Luke 14:7-11). Or again: "whoever
wishes to be great among you must be
your servant" (Matt 20:26). Or again, in
the presence of a real child whom Jesus
called and set in the midst when his disciples were concerned about the question
of the greatest in the kingdom of heaven:
"unless you change and become like
children, you will never enter into the
kingdom of heaven" (Matt 18:1-2). Or
again, in direct contrast to those who
love and claim the uppermost rooms at
feasts and the chief seats in the syna-
gogue and greetings in the market, we
are not to be called Rabbi or father or
master (Matt 23:6-7). "How can you believe when you receive glory from one of
another," is Jesus' charge against the
Jews (John 5:44); and by way of contrast, he demands that the disciples
should wash one another's feet: "For I
have set you an example, that you also
should do as I have done to you" (John
13:14-15). To come to Jesus is to take a

yoke upon oneself like a gallant ox (Matt 11:29).

All this can hardly be formulated, let alone practiced, as a general rule for improved social relationships. It is again clear that these sayings assume the existence of people who are freed by the concretely given command of Jesus from the universal dominion and constraint of ordinary conceptions of what constitutes social status and dignity and importance. It is not concealed from these people that all such conceptions are transcended and outmoded by the incursion of the kingdom of God; that there is a transvaluation of all values where the grace of God rules. They can and should reveal this in their action and abstention, in which they are no longer concerned with what those around regard as honor or dishonor. The disciple of Jesus can descend from the throne—the little throne perhaps—which even one may be allotted in human society. One does not do this willfully or of one's own choice, but as one is commanded. Yet as one is commanded one *does* it.

Force

Along a further line, the command of Jesus, and the obedience which has to be shown to it, takes the concrete form of an attestation of the kingdom of God as the end of the fixed idea of the necessity and beneficial value of force. The direction of Jesus must have embedded itself particularly deeply in the disciples in this respect. They were neither to fear force nor to exercise it. They were not to fear it as brought to bear against themselves, for at the very worst their enemies could kill only the body and not the soul. Their true and inward selves would remain inviolate. Why should they not fear, and to what degree? Because the very hairs of their head which might be hurt, and they themselves as they might be subjected to mortal attack, are all under the care of the fatherly assistance and protection of God, apart from which not even a sparrow can fall to the ground. And they are of more value than many sparrows. They may have to suffer force as it is used against them, but they are secure in face of it. Hence they are commanded: "Do not fear" (Matt 10:28-29).

On the other hand, those who have no need to fear the exercise of force against them by others because it cannot finally harm them can hardly expect to apply force against others. Should fire from heaven be called down on the Samaritan village that would not receive Jesus (Luke 9:52-53)? According to one variant only a tacit answer was given in his turning and "threatening" them. According to the other he said explicitly: "You do not know what manner of spirit you are of. For the Son of Man has not come to destroy people's lives, but to save them." And the story ends with the short statement that "they went to another village." To this there corresponds the direction given in Matt 10:13-14 that where they are not received the disciples are to shake off the dust from their feet and move on. The peace which they aim to bring to those who for the moment are obviously unworthy of it will then return to themselves (whereas they would clearly lose it if they adopted any other attitude).

Again, when the multitude came from the high priests with swords and staves as against a robber (Matt 26:47-51), and one of the disciples "put his hand on his

The Call to Discipleship   57

sword, drew it, and struck the slave of the
high priest, cutting off his ear," he was
commanded by Jesus to put the sword
back into its scabbard: "For all who take
the sword will perish by the sword" (Matt
26:52). Jesus might have had twelve le-
gions of angels from his Father. But he
does not ask for them. For he does not
need this protection and is not prepared to
make use of it. Hence the disciple who
draws his sword must be delivered from
this vicious circle. Nor does the exercise of
force begin with killing. It begins when
we are angry with our brother, when we
call him *raca* or fool, when there are judi-
cial proceedings (Matt 5:21). The disciple
of Jesus will have nothing to do with this
kind of behavior, let alone with retaliation
for the sake of glory or possession (Matt
5:38-39).

It is to be noted that in all these sayings there is no reference to the greater or
lesser atrocities usually involved in-
escapably where force is exercised. The
decisive contradiction of the kingdom of
God against all concealed or blatant
kingdoms of force is to be seen quite simply in the fact that it invalidates the
whole friend-foe relationship between

one person and another. Either way, force is the final rational *(ultima ratio)* in this relationship. If we love only those who love us again, the publicans and sinners can do the same. If we show humanity only to our brethren, the heathen do likewise (Matt 5:46-47). Of what avail is this? In spite of it, force is everywhere exercised because friend-foe relationships are not affected by it. What the disciples are enjoined is that they should love their enemies (Matt 5:44). This destroys the whole friend-foe relationship, for when we love our enemy he ceases to be our enemy. It thus abolishes the whole exercise of force, which presupposes this relationship, and has no meaning apart from it. This is attested by the disciple in what he or she does or does not do. Quite seriously and concretely he or she now drops out of the reckoning in this twofold relationship. Once again, there can be no question of a general rule, a Christian system confronting that of the world, in competition with it, and in some way to be brought into harmony with it. But again, for the one whom Jesus, in his call to discipleship, places under this particular command and prohibition, there is a concrete and incontestable direction which has to be carried out exactly as it is given. According to the sense of the New Testament, we cannot be pacifists in principle, only in practice. But we have to consider very closely whether, if we are called to discipleship, we can avoid being practical pacifists, or fail to be so.

Human Attachments

If along the third main line of the texts in question we have to do with the overcoming, proclaimed with the incursion of the kingdom of God, of the false separation between man and man revealed in the friend-foe relationship and concretely expressing itself in the exercise of force, along a fourth line we have, conversely, the dissolution of self-evident attachments between one person and another. It is a matter of what in popular usage, although not in that of the Bible, is usually described as the family. The relationships between husband and wife, parents and children, brothers and sisters, etc., are not questioned as such. One would not be human if one did not stand in these relationships. What is questioned is the

impulsive intensity with which one al-
lows oneself to be enfolded by, and thinks
that one should enfold, those who stand
to him or her in there relationships. What
is questioned is his self-sufficiency in the
warmth of these relationships, the resolv-
ing of their problems and the sphere of
their joys and sorrows. What is questioned is his imprisonment in them, in
which he is no less a captive than in other
respects he may be to possessions or
fame. The message of liberation comes to
him in this captivity to the clan. Thus the
excuse of the invited guest: "I have just
been married, and therefore I cannot
come" (Luke 14:20), is seen to be on exactly the same level as those of others
who had bought land or oxen which
claimed their prior interest. And in the
same connection Jesus gives the remark-
able reply to the man who was ready to
be a disciple but first wanted to bury his
father: "Let the dead bury their own dead:
but as for you, go and proclaim the kingdom of God" (Luke 9:59-60).

To the same series belong all the
provocative sayings of Jesus about the
leaving *(apheinai)*, dividing *(dichazein)*,
disuniting *(diamerizein)*, and even hating

(misein) which are involved in the discipleship of Jesus—not destroying the relationships as such, but certainly dissolving the connections which continually arise and obtain in them. According to Mark 10:29 we have not only to leave house and lands but even brother or sister, mother or father or children (the "or" shows us that we are dealing with individual cases), for his sake and for the sake of the Gospel. Jesus also warns us against the view that he has come to bring peace on earth (Matt 10:34-35). He has not come to bring peace, but a sword. And if a person loves father or mother, son or daughter, more than him, one is not worthy of him. Or, according to the parallel passage In Luke 12:52: "From now on five in one house will be divided, three against two and two against three." The strangest possible expression is used in Luke 14:26: "Whoever comes to me and does not hate father and mother, wife and children, and brothers and sisters, yes, and even life itself, cannot be my disciple." Hate? It is not the people that are to be hated, for why should they be excluded from the command to love our neighbors? It is the hold these people

have and by which they themselves are also gripped. It is the concentration of neighbourly love on these people, which really means its denial. It is the indolent peace of a clannish warmth in relation to these individuals, with its necessary implication of cold war against all others. The coming of the kingdom of God means an end of the absolute of family no less than that of possession and fame.

Again, there is no general rule. No new law has been set up in competition with that of the world, which points so powerfully in the opposite direction. But there is proclaimed the freedom of the disciple from the general law as it is given, and has to be exercised, in a particular situation (by the particular direction one receives). There can be no doubt that in its fear of the bogy of monasticism, Protestantism has very radically ignored this proclamation of Jesus Christ, as also that of other freedoms. To a very large extent it has acted as though Jesus had done the very opposite and proclaimed this attachment—the absolute of family. Can we really imagine a single one of the prophets or apostles in the role of the happy father, or grandfather, or even uncle, as it has found

self-evident sanctification in the famous
Protestant parsonage or manse? They may
well have occupied this role. But in the
function in which they are seen by us, they
stand outside these connections.

In this respect, too, no one is asked to
undertake arbitrary adventures. But
again, no one who really regards oneself
as called by Jesus to discipleship can
evade the question whether one might
not be asked for inner and outer obedience along these lines. The life of the new
creature is something rather different
from a healthy and worthy continuation
of the old. When the order is given to express this, we must not refuse it an obedience that is no less concrete than the
command.

Piety

Along a fifth line, to which we can never
devote too much attention, the required
obedience consists finally in a penetration of the absolute law *(nomos)* of religion, of the world of piety. It is worth
reflecting that what Jesus has in mind
was not the piety of heathen religion, but
that of the Israelite religion of revelation.

He has not, of course, come to deny or
destroy or dissolve it (Matt 5:17-18). He
himself accepts it, and he does not require
his disciples to abandon or replace it. But
he does demand that they should go a
new way in its exercise; that they should
show a "better righteousness," i.e., not
better than that of the people, the common herd, but better than that of its best
and strictest and most zealous representatives, the scribes and Pharisees; better
than the official form which it had assumed at the hands of its most competent
human champions. This better righteousness is not more refined or profound or
strict. It is simply the piety which the disciple can alone exercise in face of the im-
minent kingdom of God. It has nothing
whatever to do with religious aristocracy.
On the contrary, the kingdom knocks at
the door of the sanctuary of supreme
human worship. The disciple must act accordingly.

According to two groups of sayings
(both contained in the Sermon on the
Mount) Jesus summoned to this advance
on two different fronts. It is a matter of
morality on the one side and religion on
the other. Morality is dealt with in Matt

morality

5:21-48. The commandment: "You shall not kill," is universally accepted. But what does it mean? There is something worse than killing because it is the meaning and purpose in all killing. This is anger against one's brother; a state of contentiousness and strife. And it is here that the obedience of the disciple must begin. Again, what is meant by adultery? The real evil, from which the disciple refrains, is to be found much further back than the actual deed. It consists in the evil desire that is present prior to the act. And it is at the point of desire that we either refrain or do not refrain. Again, what is false swearing? It is all swearing because this as such is an illegitimate questioning of God. The disciple renounces this because it is enough for him if according to the best of his knowledge and with a good conscience he says either Yes or No, and not secretly both at once. What is meant by just retribution? The disciple does not exercise it in any form. What is neighbourly love? There is enjoined upon the disciple a love that includes the enemy. But, of course, when we talk like this, what becomes of the whole structure of practicable morality?

And how will its representatives and adherents react to this interpretation?

Religion is dealt with in the sayings concerning almsgiving, prayer and fasting (Matt 6:1-18), and the main drift in all of them is that these things are not to be done publicly but secretly. Where, then, is the witness?—we might ask. The answer is that the witness of the disciple consists in the fact that he refrains from attesting his piety as such. If we are to display the kingdom of God, and proclaim it from the housetops (Matt 10:27), we will not make a show of our own devoutness but keep it to ourselves, allowing God alone to be the One who judges and rewards us. This restraint will be a witness to the pious world with its continual need to publicize itself, allowing God alone to be the One who judges and rewards him. This restraint will be a witness to the pious world with its continual need to publicize itself, and perhaps even to the secular world. It will speak for itself—or rather, it will speak for that which does seriously and truly cry out for publicity. No official religiosity will readily acquiesce in the silent witness of this restraint. But here too, of course, it is not a matter of formulating and practicing principles. Nor does this twofold invasion of the sphere of common sanctity mean that a clear line of demarcation is drawn. How can we fail to see that here, too, his command refers to particular men in particular situations, demanding from them a no less particular obedience, the obedience of discipleship.

(There is another equally prominent line of concrete direction we have not yet touched upon, and shall not do so in this context. In many of the New Testament records the call to discipleship closes with the demand that the disciple should take up his cross. This final order crowns, as it were, the whole call, just as the cross of Jesus crowns the life of the Son of Man. In view of its outstanding significance we shall reserve this aspect for independent treatment.)

Looking back at what we have said about the concrete forms of discipleship, we may make the further general observation that the general lines of the call with which Jesus made men his disciples in the Gospels enable us in some sense to envisage the situations in which these men were reached by his call and how they had *the call*

to obey it concretely. Indeed, the New Testament proclamation *(kerygma)* not only permits but commands us to do this. The picture of these people and the way in which they were concretely ordered and concretely obeyed is one which ought to impress itself upon us. In this respect it forms, with the call issued by Jesus, the content of the New Testament *kerygma*.

The reason why we have to bring out these main lines along which it takes concrete shape is that the call to discipleship as it comes to us will always be shaped also by this correlated picture. Yet as it was for them, it will be a call which here today is addressed directly and particularly to each one of us, so that its specific content is not fixed by the specific content of his call there and then as we have learned it from the Gospels. To be sure, the call of Jesus will be along the lines of the encounter between the kingdom of God and the kingdoms of the world. And it will have to be accepted in this form. But this does not mean that the living Son of Man is confined as it were to the sequence of his previous encounters, or that his commanding moves only in the circle of his previous commanding and the obedience it received. It is not for us simply to reproduce those pictures. That is to say, it is not for us to identify ourselves directly with those who were called then, and therefore to learn directly from what they were commanded what we are necessarily commanded, or from their obedience what our own obedience must be. We will always know that it is his voice which calls us from the fact that in what is demanded of us we shall always have to do with a break with the great self-evident factors of our environment, and therefore of the world as a whole, which will have to be made in fact, both outwardly and inwardly, along the lines indicated in the New Testament, corresponding to, and attesting, the irruption of the kingdom of God. In other words, we shall always have to do with a form of the free activity Paul described in the imperative: "Do not be conformed to this world" (Rom 12:2).

But from what the New Testament tells us of his commanding, and of the obedience demanded from these particular people and rendered by them, <u>we have to hear his voice as he speaks to *us*, calling us in the particular situation of</u>

obedience determined by his Word. It is not enough, then, merely to copy in our activity the outlines of that in which these men had to obey his demands. This of itself is not an entry into discipleship. As we have to remember in relation to every "rule," we might try to copy everything that Jesus demanded and that these people did, and yet completely fail to be disciples, because we do not do it, as they did, at his particular call and command to us. There is, of course, no reason why he should not ask exactly the same of us as he did of them. But again—along the same lines—he may just as well command something different, possibly much more, or the same thing in a very different application and concretion. In these circumstances it might well be disobedience to be content to imitate them, for if we are to render simple obedience it must be to the One who, as he called them then, calls us today. It is now our affair to render obedience without discussion or reserve, quite literally, in the same unity of the inward and the outward, and in exact correspondence to the New Testament witness to his encounter with them. There can certainly be no question of a deviation from these main lines.

What we find along these lines can never be a mere advice of the gospel *(consilium evangelicum)*. It is always a binding mandate of the gospel *(mandatum evangelicum)* that demands the response of a corresponding decision and action. And there will always be reason for distrust against ourselves if we think that what may be required of us along these lines will be something less, or easier, or more comfortable than what we required of them. Grace—and we again recall that in the call to discipleship it is a matter of grace, of the salvation of the world, and therefore of our own salvation—cannot have become cheaper today (to use another expression of Bonhoeffer's).[6] It may well have become even more costly. Or, to put it another way, it may well be that the freedom given in and with obedience to the call to discipleship has not become less but greater. But however that may be, the freedom given in this way was then, and still is, our sanctification.

Notes

1. Barth is referring here to such works as Thomas à Kempis (1380-1471), *The Imitation of Christ.*
2. Dietrich Bonhoeffer, *Discipleship,* Dietrich Bonhoeffer Works 4 (Minneapolis: Fortress Press, 2001). German ed. 1937.
3. Gerhard Kittel, *"akoloutheō,"* in *Theological Dictionary of the New Testament,* ed. Gerhard Kittel, trans. G. W. Bromiley (Grand Rapids: Eerdmans, 1964), 1:210-16.
4. Bonhoeffer, "Simple Obedience," in *Discipleship,* 77-83.
5. Bonhoeffer, *Discipleship,* 79-80.
6. "Cheap grace is the mortal enemy of our church. Our struggle today is for costly grace." Bonhoeffer, *Discipleship,* 43.

Further Reading

Biersdorf, John E. *Healing of Purpose: God's Call to Discipleship*. Nashville: Abingdon, 1985.

Bonhoeffer, Dietrich. *Discipleship*. Edited by Geffrey B. Kelly and John D. Godsey. Translated by Barbara Green and Reinhard Krauss. Dietrich Bonhoeffer Works 4. Minneapolis: Fortress Press, 2001. Paperback edition, 2003.

Chittister, Joan. *Heart of Flesh: A Feminist Spirituality for Women and Men*. Grand Rapids: Eerdmans, 1998.

Dunn, James D. G. *Jesus' Call to Discipleship*. Understanding Jesus Today. Cambridge: Cambridge Univ. Press, 1992.

Foster, Richard. *Celebration of Discipline: The Path to Spiritual Growth*. Rev. ed. San Francisco: Harper & Row, 1988.

___. *The Challenge of the Disciplined Life: Christian Reflections on Money, Sex and Power*. San Francisco: Harper & Row, 1983.

Hall, Douglas John. *Why Christian? For Those on the Edge of Faith*. Minneapolis: Fortress Press, 1998.

Happel, Stephen, and James J. Walter. *Conversion and Discipleship: A Christian Foundation for Ethics and Doctrine*. Philadelphia: Fortress Press, 1986.

Hinson, William H. *The Power of Holy Habits: A Discipline for Faithful Discipleship*. Nashville: Abingdon, 1981.

Howard-Brook, Wes. *Becoming Children of God: John's Gospel and Radical Discipleship*. Bible and Liberation Series. Maryknoll, N.Y.: Orbis, 1994.

McKenna, Megan. *Blessings and Woes: The Beatitudes and the Sermon on the Plain in the Gospel of Luke*. Maryknoll, N.Y.: Orbis, 1999.

Moltmann, Jürgen, et al. *Communities of Faith and Radical Discipleship*. Edited by G. McLeod Bryan. Macon, Ga.: Mercer Univ. Press, 1986.

Myers, Ched. *Who Will Roll Away the Stone? Discipleship Queries for First World Christians*. Maryknoll, N.Y.: Orbis, 1994.

Norris, Kathleen. *The Cloister Walk*. New York: Riverhead, 1996.

Nouwen, Henri J. M. *Life of the Beloved: Spiritual Living in a Secular World*. New York: Continuum, 1993.

Patte, Daniel. *The Challenge of Discipleship: A Critical Study of the Sermon on the Mount as Scripture*. Harrisburg, Pa.: Trinity, 1999.

Smith, Luther E. *Intimacy and Mission: Intentional Community as Crucible for Radical Discipleship*. Scottdale, Pa.: Herald, 1994.

Storey, Peter. *With God in the Crucible: Preaching Costly Discipleship*. Nashville: Abingdon, 2002.

Wallis, Jim. *Agenda for Biblical People*. 2d ed. San Francisco: Harper & Row, 1984.

___. *The Call to Conversion*. San Francisco: Harper & Row, 1981.

___. *The Soul of Politics: A Practical and Prophetic Vision for Change*. Maryknoll, NY: Orbis, 1994.

Wink, Walter. *Jesus and Nonviolence*. Facets. Minneapolis: Fortress Press, 2003.